M000158241

Queen
of the Sky
Jackie Morris

GRAFFEG

Queen of the Sky
First published in 2015 by Graffeg Limited.

Text, photography and illustrations by Jackie Morris copyright © 2015.

Photograph page 7 © Ffion Rees
Photograph page 9 © Lynden Lomax

Designed and produced by Graffeg Limited 2020.

Graffeg Limited, 15 Neptune Court, Vanguard Way Cardiff CF24 5PJ. Wales UK. Tel 01554 824000 www.graffeg.com

Jackie Morris is hereby identified as the author of this work in accordance with section 77 of the Copyrights, Designs and Patents Act 1988.

A CIP Catalogue record for this book is available from the British Library.

All rights reserved. No part of this publication may be reproduced, stored in a retrieval system or transmitted, in any form or by any means, electronic, mechanical, photocopying, recording or otherwise, without the prior permission of the publishers.

The publisher gratefully acknowledges the financial support of this book by the Books Council of Wales. www.gwales.com

Paper from responsible sources
FSC C014138.

ISBN 9781913634599

1 2 3 4 5 6 7 8 9

Dedicated to new friends and old and those I have yet to meet. And to my beloved Mr Stenham.

With thanks to Nicola Davies and Karin Hines for reading the text and for their advice.

And special thanks to Ffion Rees for her patience with the beautiful Hiss, flying free on the wind, also her patience with me. And for understanding that I had to eat the ice cream in order to fit the day old chicks into her freezer in those very early days.

Peregrines in Pembrokeshire

Peregrines look dangerous. They are high precision engineering, shaped by natural selection to deliver death. There is something of the Exocet about them. In flight, a peregrine is the essence of wildness. Seeing one, you feel as if everything in the environment around it has been distilled, focused into this one, fast-moving body.

The presence of a peregrine is often announced by other birds. Flocks of waders put to flight, pigeons flapping wildly for cover. It is in the interest of most birds to notice a peregrine: a peregrine unnoticed is like the bullet you don't see or hear, the one that ends your life.

I've seen peregrines streaking through the mist on Scottish estuaries, silhouetted against the chalk of the Jurassic coast, materialising from a clear sky over Pembrokeshire cliffs. Every time, my heart races, my throat goes dry and I suppress the need to blink so as not to miss the smallest part of the thrill, the adrenaline rush. A few times I've seen them stoop, dropping so fast it seems they've re-calibrated gravity to afford them double the usual acceleration. They are heavy with purpose, infused with deadly will and utter fearlessness.

Peregrines are simply mesmerising: their streamlined shape; their sombre colours redolent of the uniform of some secret, crack military unit; their sublimely skilful flight, on the razor's edge between control and fierce abandon. Seeing a peregrine feels not only viscerally pleasurable but important, significant. Meaningful.

It's easy to be obsessed with such a creature. Reading J. A. Baker's book *The Peregrine* as a girl, I understood Baker's passion for the birds, his compulsion to follow and watch them. But I understood their meaning for him too: they were his conduit to the whole of the natural world, the living metaphor of the landscape and the seasons.

We humans need to feel that connection. We need to feel the tug of the umbilical cord which ties us to the Earth. Through feeling it we connect the better with each other just as babies learn to love through their first bond with their mother.

This is a story about a peregrine, about its beauty, its fierceness, but also about its meaning in the lives of two extraordinary women. Through the peregrine, they each connected more deeply with wildness, with freedom, with the wondrous loveliness of the Earth and with each other.

Nicola Davies

Nicola Davies is the award-winning author of more than 50 books for children, focussing on biological science and human relationship with the natural world. She has a lifelong love for Pembrokeshire and its wildlife.

Ramsey Island

I came to Pembrokeshire for the love of a man. Then I fell in love with the land.

I can still remember the first day, waking up, walking down the street. Bright February sunshine and the cathedral in the scoop of a valley with nothing but green fields between it and the sea. We walked all day, down to the sea and along the cliffs from Whitesands to Porth Clais. Standing on Whitesands Beach I saw Ramsey Island for the first time. A rock in the sea, two miles by one, its patchwork fields close cropped by rabbits and sheep and marked out by ancient stone walls. Farm buildings perched on the cliffs on the landward side. Between the mainland and the island, patterns of water shifted constantly. Gannets swooped and porpoise rose to cut the ceiling of the sea with black fins. We sat in late winter sunshine and talked about a future and he asked me to come and live with him in Wales, have children, be a family. I had no hesitation in saying yes.

He worked on Ramsey Island and I stayed there only twice, the first time in those early days when love was young. The peace I found there was unlike anything I had experienced before. There were visitors to Ramsey during the day but a whole island to escape into. I walked around the island and, at 4pm when the visitors left, we would scramble down steep paths to sit on beaches at the seaward side of the island where there was nothing between us and America apart from an ocean. We would lie back and watch ravens dance with the wind, the ground scented by white flowers like camomile and always the seawater seaweed iodine scent and salt.

At night on that side of the island the sky is astonishing. When there was no moon the stars texture the sky with astonishing patterns, rich and deep. I had expected it to be quiet, but in bed at night the tidal rush through the rocks called The Bitches was as loud as a motorway. And yet, because this was a sound made by nature, it didn't intrude into the peace.

I watched lapwings, sat still while a kestrel, wet from a spring shower, preened itself within feet of me. I saw stonechats and wheatears on the walls, red-bottomed bumblebees, choughs and curlew. And then there were the peregrines.

He told me that the Ramsey peregrines were reputed to be the best in all of Britain; the fiercest and fastest and prized by kings. Henry II had seen them first when he came to Pembrokeshire in 1171 on the way to Ireland. Known as Henry the Falconer because he loved the sport so, his noblemen were in the habit of taking their falcons to the table during feasts. Henry's chefs would bake pies with live songbirds in and when the pies were opened the birds did not begin to sing but flew for their lives as the noblemen unhooded their hawks. Richard II also had peregrines from Ramsey. He had a glorious mews constructed near Charing Cross in London where peregrine chicks captured from their cliff nests were taken. Peregrines from Ramsey were worth a king's ransom. They were given as gifts, they travelled to the

On quiet days you can hear time being tolled by the cathedral bells and over the fields are the twin hills of Ramsey.

crusades with Richard the Lionheart. Flying free in the skies above Ramsey they were magnificent.

The second time I stayed on Ramsey was not long after my divorce. Maddened by grief, I was working on *The Seal Children*, a story of selkies, love and loss. I spent a night on the island, sleepless, and watched the full moon rise heavy into the dark sky over the mainland, painting a silvered path across the sea connecting me to home, while seals sang haunting songs on the beaches below.

Although he had gone I wasn't alone. I still lived in my small house beside the sea where, from the back garden, you can see out across the fields to St Davids. On quiet days you can hear time being tolled by the cathedral bells and over the fields are the twin hills of Ramsey. I had two children and a dog for company and I walked the land in order to save my sanity, lost and restless in my skin. And I met and made new friends.

One of these was Ffion Rees. Born in Wales, Ffi had grown up in St Davids where she worked for Voyages of Discovery as head skipper, taking people out to experience the wonderful wildlife around the coast all summer long. Sometimes we would walk together up over the hill behind my house, my cats stalking her dog. The cats always loved to come for a walk too. Sometimes she would call and say 'come out on the boat, come away from work, the weather is beautiful.' And sometimes I would go. There was peace of mind to be found as a passenger, sitting, observing. The land looks different from the water and, for a while, as the boat pulls away from the shore you can leave behind everything with it, all the worries and work and problems.

I loved the ever-shifting patterns in the water in Ramsey Sound and seeing the cliffs in springtime, rich with swooping seabirds. It is a natural calendar, giving a real sense of time, of a world turning, of seasons with purpose. And I remember Ffion calling one day. It was late in the season, hot and, as usual, I had too much work to do.

'You haven't been out on the boats for ages. There's a few seats spare. Come on. We won't be on the water for much longer.'

I went. Around the back of the island the cliffs were golden and black with lichens. The black lichen thrives on salt spray and, when you see how high the black climbs the cliffs, you get an idea of how storm lashed they are in the winter. But this was a calm day, so warm there was no need for a coat. And on this day the air was scented with sea salt and heather, so strong and sweet you could taste it.

'The bees smell it from the mainland,' she said. 'They fly across the Sound just to get to the flowers.' And half the island was a purple glow of heather.

Within a year of my move to Pembrokeshire Ramsey Island had come up for sale. How I would have loved to have bought it. It was sold to the RSPB which seemed fitting. I have always struggled to understand the idea of ownership of land. If it belonged to anyone it belonged to the birds and the animals who lived there. And although my love for the man who brought me to this place ended, my love for the land grows stronger.

Painted soon after our first meeting. Right from the start I found her to be the most beautiful of creatures. I had never been so close to a wild peregrine for so long. Now when I look at this I recognize how ill she was, thin, almost absent, maybe feverish. Then all I saw was beauty.

Queen of the Sky

Ffion phoned.

'Are you busy?' Silence.

'Yes, I know, you're always busy. But you need to come and see what I've got in my kitchen. Just come. I'm in the hardware shop buying some gauntlets. Be careful when you go in. Don't leave the door open. And bring your camera.'

So, despite the fact that I had deadlines looming, I set off to see what it was that Ffion had in her kitchen.

I didn't realise then just how much time this would take, not just an afternoon with tea and talk, but days, then weeks and months. I had no idea that I was about to learn so much, about a friend, about a bird, about my craft. I set down my brush and drove the two miles along the quiet narrow lanes where the hawthorn trees blushed a little with ripening red berries, into town to see what it was that Ffion had in her kitchen.

It was a peregrine. A wild, adult peregrine falcon. She sat like some raggedy queen among the wreckage of potted plants she'd cleared out of the way with her battering wings, hunched, confused, alien in the domestic setting.

Ffi had bought her some chicken and was feeding her small strips of it, holding out the pieces in a pair of tweezers, wearing gardening gauntlets from Mathias' Hardware store and giving her small drops of water from a syringe.

She had flown into the sea, Ffi said, on the last but one trip of the day. Early evening, with the sea calm and the boat idling she had looked across to Ramsey and seen a peregrine flying across the North Bay on the ocean side of the island. She watched its progress as it flew lower and lower, losing height until finally it flew into the sea.

Peregrines do not swim.

Good fortune had placed Ffi and the boat in this spot. She could see the bird was alive but floundering, and she knew she could reach it and fish it out before it swallowed too much salt water.

And her good fortune was mine as well. I have loved birds ever since I began, as a child, to notice these little people of the air around me. I would walk with my dad and he would tell me their names and show me how to find their secret, hidden nests. He took me to see *Kes* at the cinema when I was older, and then I found *A Kestrel for a Knave* by Barry Hines, the book on which the film was based. Though I was slow to catch the knack of reading I loved stories and I made my way through this slim volume. *The Once and Future King* and *The Goshawk* by T. H. White held my imagination. If ever I thought of myself as an adult it was as one who lived alone in a cottage in a wood with a hawk and a hound and a horse for company.

The curious geography of my mind is filled with tales of birds; trickster ravens, thieving magpies, women with fine slate feather cloaks who turn into falcons when they wrap their cloaks around them, and swan women. Birds have threaded their flight through the backgrounds of my books, from redwings in *The Snow Whale* to lapwings in *The Cat and the Fiddle,* as I painted in winter while outside my studio the stark, cold fields filled with bright lapwings.

'What are you going to do with her?' I asked.

'I'll take her back onto the middle of the island, see if she can fly. If she's strong enough to chew her way out of the cardboard box she was in she can't have much wrong with her. In the meantime she can rest here.'

She didn't seem too stressed by being in Ffi's kitchen, so Ffion fed her and I took more photographs, making the most of being so close. I tried to fill up my eyes with the vision of her and wondered whether to ask if I could go along and watch her being set free. But I had a deadline to work towards so I set off home and went back to work.

Ragged wings, thin, earthbound. She sat on an antler with a
head filled with fierce dark thought.

The bird perched awkwardly on a curved antler in its confinement, scowling at the world and attracting the attention of the neighbourhood cats.

She didn't fly. Couldn't fly. Something was wrong with her.

I remembered another bird I had been close to, a sparrowhawk. She had flown into a window and stunned herself and someone had called to see if I might take her. She was beautiful too, with crazy eyes and a barred breast. I had walked with her up through a few of the fields above my house, arm wrapped with a towel that her claws gripped tight. I sat for a while, hoping she would lift, then stood and threw her as high as I could from my arm back up into the sky where she had come from. A short clumsy flight, then she landed awkwardly on a hedge and hunched, malevolent as only a hawk can be. I watched for a while then left, worried for her.

Two days later I found a small trail of feathers leading to her body, damp with beads of morning dew.

Back at Ffion's we talked about the bird. Her feathers were salty and Greg, the warden on Ramsey, said that she looked thin, out of condition. It doesn't take long for a bird to go into shock. There's nothing spare on a fierce hunter like this, just muscle and bone and feather. Some of her feathers seemed as if they had rotted; they were a dull brown, lifeless, with frayed edges. It looked as if she hadn't been preening. Ffion asked me to help shower the bird. Giving a peregrine a shower isn't the easiest of tasks but Ffi thought that if we could remove some of the salt remnants from her feathers the bird might begin to preen herself. There was a pattern of salt across her back from immersion in seawater, almost like watermarked damask.

Meanwhile we talked about what she might eat.

'On the island they take the rock doves,' Ffion said. 'This time of year you see them playing with the ravens. They'll take snipe, maybe woodcock, lapwings if they can and blackbirds. They learn pretty quickly not to take fulmars.'

'I know,' I said, 'I'll give Tracy a call. See what she suggests.'

Tracy, another friend, has two captive-bred owls, a barn owl and an eagle owl. It turned out that she also had a freezer full of day-old chicks. Now all we had to do was work out how many day-old chicks a peregrine might eat. We reckoned about three and so Ffion began to chop up the poor little dead things with a pair of kitchen scissors and we hoped no one would come calling because Ffion's kitchen began to look like something from a horror story. And all the time I was taking photographs, wondering what would happen next.

Even a ragged and tattered peregrine is a creature of great, wild beauty.

Perched on the grass, tethered by jesses, she turned her back to
catch the warmth from the early spring sunshine.

Ffion built a makeshift aviary in her back garden. There is only so long you can keep a peregrine in your kitchen without it starting to smell of, well, peregrine. The bird perched awkwardly on a curved antler in its confinement, scowling at the world and attracting the attention of the neighbourhood cats. I visited and watched as Ffion, her dutiful servant, carefully chopped day-old chicks into easy to swallow pieces. Now and again the bird would throw herself against the mesh of the cage, hanging from her clawed feet, her wings wide and flapping.

For the most part she just sat.

Ffion had rescued birds before; a buzzard, a guillemot chick that practiced flying by launching itself from the top of the sofa, and two peregrines that had been fulmarred. A fulmar will vomit a foul oil onto a predator who dares to get too close. This sticks its feathers together so it cannot fly. All except the guillemot chick had been sent off to the local bird hospital for recovery. So what was it about this bird that made Ffion take on the task of bringing her back to health? The other peregrines had needed immediate specialist attention to remove the fulmar oil from their feathers. Their captivity had been short, a matter of days before they were released, often from a boat near to where they had been found. Maybe it was something about this bird herself. Was it because she came from Ramsey? Maybe that was what made her special. But she may only have been journeying, a transient visitor.

Soon she seemed brighter, though feathers still ragged.
More curious, she looked around to watch the rooks in the sycamores.

This falcon knew how to pluck, shred and tidy up the corpse of a quail with a degree of skill and precision that Ffi's scissors could never hope to match.

The very name 'peregrine' derives from the Latin word, *peregrinus* meaning wanderer or foreigner. She may have been migrating before she became ill, just passing through.

Ffion's brother, Daf, suggested that Ffion talk to Rob who had a mews and aviary near Solva, home to a couple of merlin and a red-naped shaheen called Gib. This was good news for the peregrine as it turned out we were underfeeding an already starving bird. Rob visited to take a look at her and told us she was underweight, out of condition, with poor feather quality and wasted muscle. She needed a rich diet of quail to increase her weight. I wondered how on earth you chop up a quail with a pair of scissors but Rob said just to put the quail in with her, she'd know what to do. Sure enough this falcon knew how to pluck, shred and tidy up the corpse of a quail with a degree of skill and precision that Ffi's scissors could never hope to match.

I think Ffion asked Rob if he fancied taking on the bird himself. He said no, he was busy, but he would help if he could. He had a space in the mews, a larger space where she could perch up high, move more freely, rest and feed. There were decisions to be made and it seemed they boiled down to three choices. Ffion could do what I had done with the sparrowhawk and let her go now to take her chances, which would be slim. She would probably be fox food in a day or two. Or she could work with her to bring on her plumage, build up her muscle and fly her. It would take time and patience, long hours, hard work, and may not, in the end, be successful, but at least when she was released she would be flying fit and able to hunt, chase and kill again. The other alternative was to send her to a falconry centre where she could be used as a breeding bird and where she would be captive, caged. The decision was made. Ffion sought and was granted a license by DEFRA to keep the wild bird for a period of time in an attempt to rehabilitate and release her back to the sky.

I visited the mews a few times, to see her again.

Rob has a large aviary with fancy pheasants and other birds, as well as a mews with a hawk or two and an injured buzzard. The mews is part of the grounds of a large old house near Solva, the drive lined by a copse of tall trees where rooks roost in the evenings. The autumn leaves were fast falling now, revealing the casual architecture of the rookery high up in the branches. There's an office, a walled garden courtyard. It's sheltered, but near the cliffs. There is a sense of being high up, near the sea.

The falcon was like a magnet for me, drawing me away from my studio. I had already made a large painting of her based on the first days of meeting her. Watching her, even for these few weeks, I could see how much she was changing. She sat high in her cage, watchful, more confident, more aware. By now Ffion would take in a whole pigeon or half a quail. There was no need to chop it up, she was perfectly capable of ripping apart whatever was placed before her.

The falcon often bathed in a large shallow dish of water and preened her feathers which had lost some of their ragged brownness. To be close to her was a gift. She was so beautiful, she filled the eye, and the heart. But she looked so wrong, sitting in the cage, waiting, brooding.

Outside the weather for wild hawks was awful. It had changed in a matter of days from being a mellow autumn of sunshine and gold leaves to storms like there hadn't been for years. The sea lashed at the land, angrily tearing, peeling back beaches to reveal remnants of ancient forests and shipwrecks that had lain undisturbed for centuries beneath feet of sand. On Whitesands Beach near St Davids graves were uncovered, reputed to be those of the first ever Christian missionaries, buried beside the beach in slate-slatted coffins. High tides joined forces with storms and the results were spectacular scenes of flooding and erosion.

Meanwhile the birds, crouched and huddled in bushes for shelter, were thrown around in the sky whenever they rose up, hungry, to hunt. Seabirds

'She's fitter now, Jac,' Ffion said. 'Moving towards flying again.'

perished in hundreds, fragile bodies washed up on the shore. In her cage the peregrine was sheltered and well fed. But she wasn't flying.

I spent the next couple of weeks travelling through Wales and England, talking about books, painting in bookshops. The next time I saw the peregrine it was early in the New Year and she had been moved to the weatherings, a falconry term for an area where the hawk is tethered but more open to the sky. She was wearing jesses, leather cuffs around her feet tethering her to a line. I'd seen captive-bred birds before, even flown a Harris hawk, yet to see her, a wild bird, bound and restrained went against all my natural instincts. But then I remembered where my instincts had led when it came to the beautiful sparrowhawk.

'She's fitter now, Jac,' Ffion said. 'Moving towards flying again. Her feathers are beginning to moult through. That's why we had to put the jesses on. So she can be handled and we can weigh her'

I wished I had been there to watch the process.

Sitting in the garden, the rooks calling from the treetops, the clipped lawn on the courtyard green from winter rain we sat in the cold clear sunshine of the new year drinking tea, watching the clouds, talking.

'First we had to catch her. It wasn't easy,' Ffion told me. 'She's kind of ok with me, suspicious of anyone else. Anyway, we caught her with a net, then Rob hooded her to make her easier to handle. He put the leather cuffs around her legs and then we tried to weigh her, but she wouldn't sit. She just went limp, like a dead bird, hanging from her jesses, not even flapping.'

"So what happens now?" I asked.

Ffi looked across to the tumbled down wall of the weatherings.

'Well, I have to get her to fly across the cage and sit on my glove.'

We watched the sun sinking. As it went behind the wall the temperature dropped.

It sounded easy. One hawk, tethered in a weathering, represented quite a big step forward from where we had been. But from that day both Ffion and the falcon's training really began.

Ffion named her Hiss after the noise she made when she was not particularly pleased and, day after day, Ffi would go and sit with her for a while talking, whistling and bringing chicks, or maybe a bit of pigeon. Day after day she would move a little closer and day after day Hiss would sit and scowl. To train
a hawk to the glove you have to keep it hungry, but Ffion is a kind soul and found this hard. So day after day she would sit, arm extended away from her body, with a chick, a small piece of quail, or the leg of a turkey chick held in gloved hand.

Day after day.

She had looked beautiful when she first arrived. Now her feathers began to take on the blue sheen of good health, and her eye the wild glint of freedom.

As I watched from the side-lines a level of trust was growing between woman and bird, a measure of confidence in each other.

After a few weeks Hiss flew across her enclosure, snatched the chick, took it back to her perch and, with her back turned, grudgingly ate it. By this time her feathers were moulting out and blue-grey was beginning to show through the brown. Damaged feathers were falling away, the blue feathers were stronger. Her health was improving.

Now and again I would go to the weatherings and watch, standing and waiting, listening to the rooks bicker in the treetops, waiting for the falcon to fly. But Hiss was nervous, spooked by anyone other than Ffi. It was best in a way that she respond only to one person. There was no good reason to have her become accustomed to people and so very many reasons to keep as much of her wild mistrustful nature as she could.

Day after day after day, until the day she landed on Ffion's glove and sat and ate. As I watched from the sidelines a level of trust was growing between woman and bird, a measure of confidence in each other. Now some days she would come and sit on the hand and stay, even when she had finished her food. Some days she would refuse and Ffion would have to walk away and come back later, leaving her hungry. And so, after a while, she would come to the glove as a matter of course. Then one fine spring day when the air was still and the sun warm, Ffi lifted the bird, and with her tied by her jesses to a loop on the glove, she walked out into the sunshine. This was the time for Hiss to learn to ride on the glove and for Ffion to learn the art of tying falconry knots with one hand (the other being rather busy carrying the weight of the hawk.)

For some part of each day Ffi would go to the weatherings, whistle to Hiss and tempt her to the glove with a tasty, ghoulish treat, then carry her out and walk a while, or tether her to a perch in the garden where she could stretch wings and feel the sun on her feathers. At such times it was easy to see how the relationship between the two was growing.

She rode on the glove like a medieval queen, testing her wings.

They seemed at ease with each other. The falcon, more beautiful than ever as she moved towards health, looking around at the world with wild eyes, watching every movement, alert for the whir of flight overhead. She rode on the glove like a medieval queen, testing her wings.

Now she would sit on the scales to be weighed, albeit reluctantly.

Now it was time for her to begin to fly. The dark days of winter were passing and spring came in, warm and wonderful with clear skies and settled seas. The beaches still wore the scars of the powerful storms and each day the sand was shifting, making new patterns, uncovering ancient woodland, tree stumps, fossils.

With Rob's help Ffion erected a creance; a perch, quite high, with a long wire to which the hawk would be tethered by a thin thread and a swivelled ring. Rob gave Ffion the basic information she needed to take the next steps towards independence for the bird. The idea was to carry Hiss to the creance, put her on the perch, back off a few steps and then call her to the glove where a small treat of fresh flesh awaited her. This was outside. A wide open ploughed field with so many distractions for a bird who had wintered in the weatherings, seeing only Ffion, Rob and, now and again, me. What would she do? Would she try to fly away? She couldn't, because the thin leash and swivel would only allow her to fly along the creance.

Ffion whistled, held out the chick, stood still, waiting, hoping. And Hiss flew, along the line to land on the glove. Just a short flight, a very short flight, but she did it.

At first it wasn't much further than she had flown across the pen in the weatherings, but over a few weeks Ffion tried ten yards, then twenty. I went to watch, walking out beside them on a sunny day. By now the creance had been moved round to the other side of the mews and the office. We walked over an area of boggy ground, through a gate, where I let Hiss and Ffion go through first so as not to spook the hawk. The trees were all winterbone branches still, the bright sun picking out nests where rooks were beginning to squabble over brittle sticks, remaking nests ready to lay eggs. Ffion attached Hiss to the looped wire, placed her on the perch, then turned and walked away. She took half a chick out from her hawking pouch, placed it in the glove, held out her arm and whistled.

Hiss rose immediately from the cross of wood and seemed to hang for a moment before stretching wide her wings to push against the air. Then, fast as lightning, she flew, stretched out her clawed feet, and landed on the glove.

Perfect.

Each flight strengthened muscles and saw her closer to freedom. Sometimes I tried to photograph her in flight, crouching low to frame her against the blue spring sky. Other-times I just watched the wings beat the air, the hawk rise, the fast dash, the lift and stretching out of clawed feet to land, light on the glove.

Each flight saw her closer to the day she would fly free.

Just a short flight, a very short flight, but she did it.

She was not always so textbook perfect in her lessons. She soon learned what the movement of Ffion's hand to the bag meant, and as fast as Ffion's fingers found the food Hiss would be flying, before the whistle to call her. I would call to let Ffion know she was on the way and Ffi would turn fast and lift her hand for the bird to land.

She flew, still tethered to the ground, but still she flew and as she did so it seemed the earth stood still and all sound dropped away. This is what she was made for. She was the queen of the sky, beauty incarnate. And if sometimes she landed on Ffion's head rather than the glove, well, Ffi soon learned it was best to wear a hat.

First flights, tethered on a creance, called with a whistle,
low to the ground. Progress.

In Ffion I saw adoration of a wild thing. In the bird there was at times the curious sense of wild humour.

I watched Ffion, I watched the bird, and I watched the trust grow between them. In Ffion I saw adoration of a wild thing. In the bird there was at times the curious sense of wild humour. If the weather was bright Ffi loved to bring her back to the weatherings via the office and the windows that would act like
a mirror. Hiss would catch sight of her reflection and see another peregrine staring back at her, fluffing up her feathers to make herself as big as big as she possibly could as a challenge to her beautiful self.

I began to worry. So much time, patience and effort had been invested and a close relationship had formed between woman and bird. And the next stage would be free flight. Would Ffion be able to fly her free? Would she return, or, if offered, would she take her freedom too soon perhaps? Although she was stronger now she was far from flying fit, as she would need to be in order to hunt, pursue, and kill for herself.

A wild peregrine will often hunt by finding a perch, high on a cliff and scan around until it finds its feathered food. They have been known to fly at speeds of 180 -200 miles an hour. Not every hunt is successful. Sometimes they miss. Sometimes a hunt can end in disaster. I have a friend who found the still warm body of a young peregrine lying on a pebble bank beside the sea. There was not a mark on the bird to show how it had died, but a few feet away was the body of a blackbird, and clutched in the peregrine's claws were a few fine feathers from the blackbird's breast. The two birds lying so close told the story of a failed hunt, of a bird misjudging the height and stooping straight into the ground, a head on collision at 180 miles an hour. The body of the peregrine was taken to a vet to certify the cause of death - peregrines are protected birds and it is illegal to kill one - and then to a taxidermist. This peregrine now flies forever, caught in a pose, lifting a jewelled necklace.

One beautiful day I had another call from Ffion.

'I flew her, Jac. I flew her free, just for a few minutes. She came back.'

As Ffion talked I could hear the joy in her voice.

'I didn't have the courage to plan it. I knew it was time. I was scared. Scared she might not come back. That I would let her go and she would realise that she wasn't tied and be away. So, I took her out and was going to tie her on the creance again, then we stood for a while in the field.'

It was quiet. I waited to hear more.

'She flew. It was such a clear calm day I thought, it's now or never. Days like this, without the wind. So few. She had flying jesses on, just in case. I feared she would go once she knew she was free. That would be it. Didn't want her to end up tangled in a tree. But she flew. And she came back.'

Wonderful news. My heart gave a little kick of envy. She's done it. Even though it was just that once and not very far Hiss still flew free, straight to the glove.

"I don't think she even knew she was free," Ffion said. But I thought she did. Or maybe she just hunted straight for the nearest food. As a falcon would.

I began to work on a painting of Hiss flying free.

Her first free flight, spreading her wings into the clear blue.

Once, in those times when Ffion flew Hiss free, she did lose her.

I went to watch them flying, walking out with them into the ploughed field to where the old cannon stood. I stayed back, crouched low against the hedge, keeping still so as not to distract the hawk and watched as the bird threw herself into the sky and swooped down onto the swinging lure - a kind of leather sandbag with part of a bird fixed tightly to it, swung round and around to mimic prey. Again only a short flight, then Ffion brought her back, nervous of losing her. But her strength was building now.

She did exercises with her, making her jump from the ground to the fist to strengthen her leg and wing muscles. Birds of prey are most vulnerable when they are on the ground, eating. They need to be able to rise into the relative safety of the sky, fast and furious, away from other predatory birds and foxes. Hiss leapt to the glove from the ground again and again, heaving herself up with strong wings. A huge helicopter came low across the fields, one of those military things with double rotor blades. She didn't even seem to notice.

They were so comfortable with each other now that Ffion stroked the back of her head and the feathers on her back and I must admit to feeling envious of this wonderful, close relationship between woman and bird. Yet I was also glad to be here on the edge of it, watching, learning. Part of me so wanted to hold her, glove on my hand, to feel the weight of the bird, the lift of her wings. But I knew that Hiss didn't need to be held by me. The only human in her life was Ffion, and one was enough.

Once, in those times when Ffion flew Hiss free, she did lose her. They went through the usual routine. Ffion placed the bird on the cannon and walked away. Then she whistled and swung the lure and Hiss lifted, high, high, up in to the sky and took off, over the hedge and off to the cliffs. Maybe she heard a bird call. Maybe another peregrine. For five minutes Ffion called, whistled, swung the lure and walked to the edge of the field. Five long minutes. And then Ffion thought to herself, 'well, that's it, after all that she's chosen her time to go.'

One by one she took off the jesses that tethered the bird to her, cutting off the leather cuffs, tucking them in her pocket.

And then she came back, flying over the edge, fast as a bullet, down from the sky and onto the lure and Ffi fixed her back on to the thin thread that clipped her to her belt. She had come back. But better still she had flown, further than she had since her first days in captivity; strong, high and free.

Days went by. Day after still calm day of waking to blue sky and birdsong. Blackthorns blossomed outside the window. Swallows returned.

I had hoped to be there at the end, to see what happened next, but as things turned out I was far away. I had driven across Wales, across to the other side of England, to the coast of Norfolk and Suffolk, where I was sitting in fields watching hares, beneath trees listening to nightingales.

Ffion phoned.

'She's gone,' she said.

It had been a beautiful day and Ffion had been on the boats. In the early evening she went to the weathering, called Hiss to the glove and walked out to where the old rusty cannon rose up out of the ploughed field on the cliffs above the sea.

One by one she took off the jesses that tethered the bird to her, cutting off the leather cuffs, tucking them in her pocket. Hiss wouldn't need them anymore.

As Ffion spoke I imagined the bright clear evening light, and the sky going golden as the sun began to set.

'I gave her a whole pigeon. I wanted to send her off with a good feed. She sat on the cannon, I put the pigeon at her feet and walked away to the edge of the field to watch.'

'Hiss ate the pigeon. She took her time, stopping now and again to look around. Some crows flew over, but she just carried on eating. The light began to fade from the day. A fox wandered by, I think I surprised him.'

'Then, without a backward glance she took off. I had hoped she would roost in the trees by the office, but she took off the way she had on that other day, over the field, across the hedge, off to the cliffs.'

I could see it all from the way she spoke. I could hear the quiet sadness in her voice.

'I cried a lot.' she said.

So did I, just a little as, on the other side of the country, my heart lifted with her. I had been so lucky to get so close to a wild peregrine; to photograph, to draw, to paint. Watching the relationship develop between woman and bird had been wonderful. Ffion hadn't set out to master the wild nature of the bird, to tame her. She had taken this fragile, sick bird, brought her back to

A wish. That she will fall on her prey like death from the sky and
always catch a friendly wind.

The next morning Ffion went back to the field and called for a while but no bird came.

health and, with time and patience, given her back her wings and her freedom. Finally, she had given her back to the sky.

The next morning Ffion went back to the field and called for a while but no bird came. I messaged her, to hear if there was any sign, but no, she had gone.

For a few days Rob put some food out on the cannon and sometimes it went. But he couldn't say whether Hiss had taken it.

Once, a few weeks later, Ffion spotted a peregrine, slightly shabby with tattered tail feathers, around the north side of Ramsey. She said she liked to think that it could have been Hiss. But there was no way of really knowing.

It took real courage to love a wild thing so much and then to let her go. When I spoke to Ffion about this later she said she always knew that Hiss didn't 'belong' to her. Although she had come to her like a gift from the sky Hiss had always been on loan from the wild. Time and chance and maybe the wild gods had placed Ffion's boat in just the right place and turned her sharp eyes in the right direction at that moment so that she saw the bird fail and fall. Time and chance. And maybe the wild gods.

If she had kept her, what would her life have been? To sit in the weatherings, perched and tethered for most of the day? To be flown for half an hour and fed like a dog? No. That's no life for something born to freedom and the wild. So she had been set free to take her chances back in the sky where she belonged, dark death on fierce wings.

A wild peregrine in a mews is a beautiful thing. But a wild peregrine in a mews leaves a hole in the sky.

Ffion had quickly learned lessons, from the first days of showering a peregrine and chopping up chicks with a pair of kitchen scissors to walking the fields with a hawk on the glove and whistling her down from the sky with a lure dancing in the air. But I had learned too, from a distance, about handling a hawk, but also about friendship. It takes a lifetime to find your true friends, your tribe, in this busy crowded world. Friendship isn't a casual thing. It's precious. And I was so proud of my friend for what she had achieved with this one wild and precious thing.

A hope. That she will never go hungry. Wild. Free. Beauty.

Watching her fly. The earth stood still. I forgot to breathe. Everything else fell away until there was just a shape of a peregrine. Nothing else. Just her.

For me it was weeks and months of painting as the shape of the bird haunted my dreams

In my time with Hiss I had learned something of the shape of a peregrine falcon. When you wish to draw or paint something, the very best way is to draw from life, to look at the thing, see the space it takes up and watch it move in the world. I had thought her beautiful from the very first moment I saw her, hunched and grumpy in the kitchen. I watched as she changed from a dour sick thing to a strong healthy bird, feathers casting off their dull, rotten brown with sea salt watermarks to become a deep slate blue. She still had a ragged edge about her, her tail was still tattered, but when she flew she was something to behold. She would sit on the glove, look around at the world that she knew was hers.

A simple phone call from a friend, "Come and see what I've got in my kitchen." I almost said that I didn't have time, that I was too busy working. Almost. For Ffion it was months of patience, working to send her home to the sky. For me it was weeks and months of painting as the shape of the bird haunted my dreams, both waking and sleeping, then trying to catch the story in order to share it.

Why?

Because it is beautiful.

Because I know that other people will be touched by the wild heart of the bird and the courage of the one who loved her fiercely enough to let her go.

Because some stories just demand to be told.

My wish for her is that she
always hunt well, that the wind
is kind to her, that she find a
mate and a home. Pilgrim bird.

All that remains are
memories of a wild thing,
two broken feathers and the
tethers that bound her to
perch and glove.

Other books published by Graffeg:

The Quiet Music of Gently Falling Snow
Jackie Morris

Geiriau Diflanedig
Robert Macfarlane, Jackie Morris
and Welsh adaptation by Mererid Hopwood

The Ice Bear
Jackie Morris

The Snow Leopard
Jackie Morris

Tell Me a Dragon
Jackie Morris

Ga' i Hanes Draig
Jackie Morris
Welsh adaptation by Mererid Hopwood

Cat Walk
Jackie Morris

Ramsey Island and Beyond
Ffion Rees